★State Government★

Karen Kenney

rourkeeducationalmedia.com

Before Reading:

Building Academic Vocabulary and Background Knowledge

Before reading a book, it is important to tap into what your child or students already know about the topic. This will help them develop their vocabulary, increase their reading comprehension, and make connections across the curriculum.

1. Look at the cover of the book. What will this book be about?
2. What do you already know about the topic?
3. Let's study the Table of Contents. What will you learn about in the book's chapters?
4. What would you like to learn about this topic? Do you think you might learn about it from this book? Why or why not?
5. Use a reading journal to write about your knowledge of this topic. Record what you already know about the topic and what you hope to learn about the topic.
6. Read the book.
7. In your reading journal, record what you learned about the topic and your response to the book.
8. After reading the book complete the activities below.

Content Area Vocabulary
Read the list. What do these words mean?

budget
constitution
enacts
federalist
industry
reflect
representative
senators
vital
wages

After Reading:

Comprehension and Extension Activity

After reading the book, work on the following questions with your child or students in order to check their level of reading comprehension and content mastery.

1. How are representatives under a state government different from representatives under the federal government? (Asking questions)
2. State laws differ from state to state. Why? (Infer)
3. What are some things that the federal government can do that the state government cannot? (Summarize)
4. How has your state government impacted your life? (Text to self connection)
5. Explain the duties of the state government. (Summarize)

Extension Activity

Explore your state! Create a state brochure about your state. Research who your governor is, where your state capital is, who your district representative is, and other fun facts about your state. You can draw or print pictures that represent your state. Share your brochure with your classmates.

Table of Contents

★ What Is a State Government? ★

A terrible tornado rips through Oklahoma. Parts of the state become disaster zones. The state's governor calls upon the National Guard to help the state's people. The soldiers rescue others and clean up the state. This is just one of the many powers of state governments.

A state government is the governing body of a state. It **enacts** and enforces laws specific to a state. It creates a state's **budget**, too. Funding schools and fixing roads are some of a state government's responsibilities.

The United States has a **federalist** government. This means its powers are split between states and the national government. This system was created when the United States became an independent nation in 1776. The colonies already had their own governments. So the U.S. Constitution allowed the new states to keep some government powers. And it gave the federal government control over other powers.

The U.S. Constitution defines how the U.S. government works.

Before the U.S. Constitution, each colony made its own paper money. The federal government later took over this power. Benjamin Franklin printed Philadelphia's three pence bill in 1764.

Federal and state governments have a lot in common. They each have three branches of power and a **constitution**. The branches check each other's powers. No branch can have too much power.

A state constitution defines how a state government works. It is very similar to the U.S. Constitution. The branches of power and rules for local governments are outlined in a state's constitution.

The Utah State Senate is part of the state government's legislative branch.

A state governor leads the executive branch. A state's citizens elect the governor. This person serves a certain term in office. A governor also has a staff. Other leaders help run the executive branch.

New Jersey Government

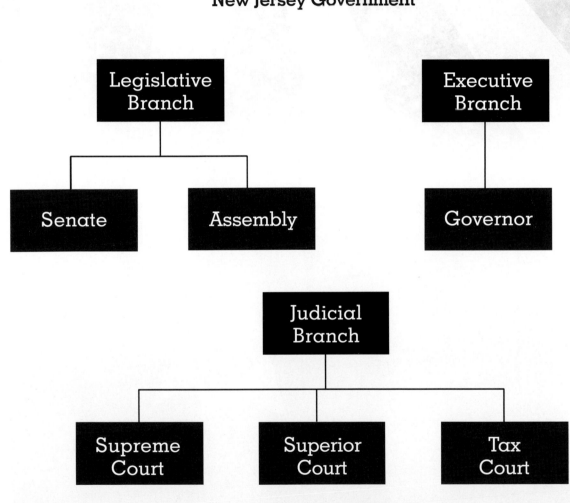

The New Jersey government is organized with an executive, legislative, and judicial branch. Most state governments are organized this way.

A state's legislative branch creates state laws. Most states have two houses in their legislative branch. One house is the Senate. The other house is usually called the House of Representatives, but some states call it the Assembly or House of Delegates. Each **representative** is elected to serve the needs of people in certain parts of the state.

Each state also has a judicial branch. This branch enforces laws. The highest court is a state's Supreme Court. Below this are the lower courts.

Judges are a part of the judicial branch of government.

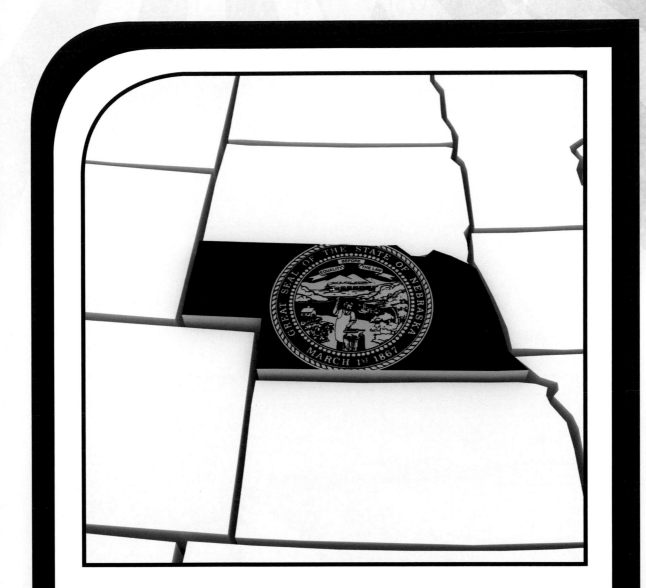

Nebraska is the only state with one legislative house.
This also means it has fewer **senators** than other states.

★ State Government's Role ★

The United States is a huge country. Different states have different needs. Each one makes laws to suit its land and people.

Arizona is a hot and dry state. Its government has many laws about water use. In Maine, snow and ice can create problems in the winter. This state has laws about removing snow. State laws also **reflect** the history and culture of a state.

Canals bring water to dry areas of the state of Arizona.

State governments have limited powers. Some things are completely under state control, such as education and **industry**. Some powers are shared with the federal government. For example, both the state and federal government collect taxes.

Citizens pay taxes to their state government.

However, there are some powers that go beyond state control. Only the federal government can print money and declare war.

Famous State Governors

Some state governors have become famous across the United States. Ambrose Burnside was a general in the U.S. Civil War. He also served as the governor of Rhode Island from 1866 to 1869.

Burnside became well-known for his unusual facial hair. Because of this governor, side whiskers became known as sideburns.

Burnside, seated in the center, alongside the officers of the 1st Rhode Island at Camp Sprague, in 1861.

Ambrose Burnside
1824–1881

California's former governor was famous long before he served. Arnold Schwarzenegger was a famous movie star and athlete.

Schwarzenegger held the governor's office from 2003 to 2011. He focused on improving job **wages** and air quality in the state. He also worked with the Special Olympics.

Former California Governor Arnold Schwarzenegger won the title of Mr. Universe in 1967 for his training as a bodybuilder.

State governments have important roles in states. Their three branches share power. Their laws fit the needs of the land and their people. They control education and other **vital** services. And they can bring help quickly to people in need. How does your state government help you?

Glossary

budget (BUHJ-it): a plan for how to earn and spend money

constitution (kon-stuh-TOO-shuhn): the system of laws in a state or a country that outline personal rights and ways to govern

enacts (in-AKTS): put a law into effect

federalist (FED-ur-uhl-ist): a country that has both national and state governments and shares powers

industry (IN-duh-stree): the group of businesses and factories that make products in an area

reflect (ri-FLEKT): evidence of the past that can be seen or understood in something today

representative (rep-ri-ZEN-tuh-tiv): a person who is elected to speak for people from a certain area of a state or country

senators (SEN-it-orz): the people who work in a state's or country's senate

vital (VHY-tuhl): something essential or necessary

wages (WEYJZ): amount paid to a person for the work they do

Index

Show What You Know

1. What are the three branches of a state government?
2. Why does the author explain that Arizona has water restriction laws?
3. Why were states given government powers when the nation was founded?
4. What does a state governor do?
5. How has your state government helped you?

Websites to Visit

bensguide.gpo.gov/3-5/index.html

kids.usa.gov/learn-about-the-states

www.state.nj.us/hangout_nj/government.html

About the Author

Karen Latchana Kenney is the author of more than 80 books for children. She's written about many forms of government and U.S. symbols, like the White House and the American bald eagle. Kenney lives in Minneapolis, Minnesota.

Meet The Author!
www.meetREMauthors.com

PHOTO CREDITS: page 4 ©Fotolotti; page 6 © zimmytws; page 7 © Public Domain, Wikipedia; page 10 © bikeriderlondon; page 11 © Tatiana Kalashnikova; page 12 © Jim W. Parkin; page 13 © Moustyk; page 14 © Btazej Tyjak; page 15 © Rossella Apostoli; page 16, 17 © Library of Congress; page 18 © Getty Images/David McNew; page 20 © Bart Sadowski, negaprion; page 21 © ericfoltz, trekandshoot, jerry2313

Edited by: Jill Sherman

Cover by: Nicola Stratford, nicolastratford.com
Interior design by: Jen Thomas

Library of Congress PCN Data

State Government/ Karen Kenney
 (U.S. Government and Civics)
  ISBN 978-1-62717-683-5 (hard cover)
  ISBN 978-1-62717-805-1 (soft cover)
  ISBN 978-1-62717-921-8 (e-Book)
Library of Congress Control Number: 2014935459

Also Available as:

Printed in the United States of America, North Mankato, Minnesota